atomic morals

mia rose everson

BookLeaf
Publishing

Presentation by *BookLeaf Publishing*

Web: www.bookleafpub.com

E-mail: info@bookleafpub.com

ISBN: 9789395620949

First edition 2022

ACKNOWLEDGEMENT

Mitchell Gardner, my year 10 English teacher has pushed and encouraged me more than anyone else. Mr Gardner has taught me above and beyond satisfactory. He never failed to believe in me and my ideas. I cannot thank him enough for the way he has led me through the worst year I have had to endure so far.

I would like to acknowledge the people who have hurt, inspired and built the person I am today; without them I would have not a thing to write about.

t

my body and my pride
were no longer mine
you had taken my last cent of incentive
and left me defenceless.
fragile with a newfound confidence
within myself
built from rock bottom
the lowest was you

j

he was undeniably
my temporary escape
my circumstantial reoccurrence
the unknowing manipulator
but, he was mine
my past, my forever first love

b

was it your celestial scent
or mine
that gravitates us together
every now and then
you're not that special -
but then again
i'm smiling as i type
this poem about you

0400

i've never been so scared of myself.
his number dialled,
intoxicated.
my physical - demolished,
arrested.

the voice within

as she woke
the reminder she set for herself
night, after sleepless night
took control.
go for a walk, go for a walk.
go for a run...

22/12/21

i will forever feel disgusting
when i picture your tall, masculine image
or the straight black jeans
i wore on the blue beach box
that agonizing summer night
bound to happen
i should've known.
because in the end, "i wanted it"

the beginning of the end

if the sun were to cease
then would begin
the termination of all
8 minutes 20 seconds
the last photon
on its way to resurrect earth
for the very last time.
then comes the finale,
of what was once popularly
known as 'the milky way'

7 words, 2 souls

little did he know
his spoken words
defeat her unspoken notions
nor will he ever;
3am, perhaps at noon
undoubtedly she would reflect
on where she went wrong
in her role as his little girl
his "tiny dancer"

neurodivergent

constantly craving stimulation
to learn something new
mental or physical
sustaining much more than enough
but somehow left
with less than a feeling
and more of a void

atoms

i tend to get bored
so incredibly bored
in my mind as it's racing
round and around
although, i'm simply surrounded
by nothing besides everything

interstellar

i want to be loved
like the moon and the stars,
i want to fall in love
and for it to be nothing but interstellar

i want to be admired
by him and his eyes
all the little children
with their not so silent cries

i want to be respected
but not seen as a threat,
i want to be able
to make the most loving of friends

but most importantly,
i want to love myself;
the way i love sunsets
the chirps from the trees
the stupid little talks
like the birds and the bees

i want to love myself
so i can be free
from the burden that haunts

my soul, and the girl
who really isn't me

maybe, i'll be everything i desire
the person i was, prior the fire
internally lit,
into an inevitable abyss
everlasting trauma, i unruly reminisce

but something inside
is holding me back

bleeding ink

betrayal
the worst genre of heartbreak
unforgivingly vile

the power of a pinky
the depth of a promise
cracked in your words
broken in your actions

the link of my pinky
intertwined with yours
meant nothing to you

teen

thirteen
i was so very young
fourteen
the self hatred begun
fifteen
i grew a strong resentment towards my mum
and sixteen
am barely holding on

be honest

"i'm fine"
means i'll tell you what's wrong
the sixth time you ask
but you only ever ask five
so i groan and exhale
until you ask again,
when you do
i'm far too embarrassed
to bring attention to the problem
to the problem which you knew

repetition repetition repetition

repetition
oh, how i hate it
how i mumble my words
oh, how i hate it
but will inevitably say it quieter
oh, how i hate it
quieter, so you can't hear
oh, how i hate it
nothing but my insignificance

red

the colour of this jumper
the shade of my lips
the way he makes me feel
burning with red
angry all over with no disguise
i am red and red am i

jade

i wonder what she's like
i wonder what she likes
i wonder what would've happened
if she could've stayed
maybe in another lifetime
maybe never
i know she knows me
i wish i knew her
i wonder what she's like

fearless

when you look inside
and dig deep down
the fear of dying is
consequently,
the dissatisfaction with the way
one lived on earth
in the physical realm

www.ingramcontent.com/pod-product-compliance
Lightning Source LLC
Chambersburg PA
CBHW070732160726
48003CB00006BA/2461